Girlfriends

handmade gifts
from the heart

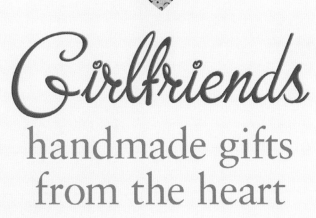

Post Card ~

This Space For Writing Messages

Dearest Sarah,
I can't tell you
how much your gift
meant to me,
... well all the
... that the
... well.

Sarah Smith
2924 Everett Rd.

Place
Stamp Here
Domestic
One cent
Foreign
Two cents

Girlfriends

handmade gifts
from the heart

by Taylor Hagerty

Sterling Publishing Co., Inc. New York
A Sterling/Chapelle Book

Credits

If you have any questions or comments, please contact:

Chapelle, ltd., Inc.,
P.O. Box 9252, Ogden, UT 84409
(801) 621-2777 (801) 621-2788 Fax
e-mail: chapelle@chapelleltd.com
Web site: www.chapelleltd.com

A Red Lips 4 Courage book
Red Lips 4 Courage Communications, Inc.
8502 E. Chapman Ave., 303
Orange, CA 92869
Web site: www.redlips4courage.com

Library of Congress Cataloging-in-Publication Data available

10 9 8 7 6 5 4 3 2
Published by Sterling Publishing Co., Inc.
387 Park Ave. South, New York, NY 10016
©2005 Taylor Hagerty
Distributed in Canada by Sterling Publishing
c/o Canadian Manda Group, 165 Dufferin St.
Toronto, Ontario, Canada M6K 3H6
Distributed in Great Britain by Chrysalis Books Group PLC,
The Chrysalis Building, Bramley Road, London W10 6SP, England
Distributed in Australia by Capricorn Link (Australia) Pty. Ltd.
P.O. Box 704, Windsor, NSW 2756, Australia
Printed and Bound in China
All Rights Reserved

Sterling ISBN 1-4027-1609-5

For information about custom editions, special sales, premium and corporate purchases, please contact Sterling Special Sales Department at 800-805-5489 or specialsales@sterlingpub.com

The Art of Giving

If it's made with your hands, it comes from your heart.

Like great gardening, the art of giving reaps a rich harvest. While the gardener delights in a summer parade of hollyhocks and roses, sweet peas and daisies, what we cultivate when we give of ourselves is a future bright with friends.

Our oldest and dearest girlfriends are like the perennials, whose bright countenances lift our spirits year after year. Then there are annuals —the new friends we meet when we take a class or cart the kids to soccer. Of course, there are always the seeds that surprise us—those friends who seem to pop out of nowhere like a delightful volunteer snapdragon or marigold.

Just like our favorite flowers, our friendships must be nurtured. Love and companionship provide the good soil, sunlight, and soft rain friendships need to grow vibrant and strong. Tending to our girlfriends as we would a garden is sometimes as simple as lending

an ear, a cup of sugar, or an hour of babysitting when she needs it most.

But at other times, we have the privilege of helping our friends through valleys of sorrow or moments of pure joy—a birthday, a new baby, a wedding. With times like these in mind, we wanted to create a book to give girlfriends plenty of great gift-giving ideas, perfect for any occasion.

Because we believe the old-fashioned notion that everything handcrafted comes from the heart, each of these projects has a timeless feel she's sure to cherish. From gift wrap to beadwork, pillows, purses, and more, we have no doubt you'll find our ideas inspiring, whether you have only an extra hour to spare, or a day or more.

So pour yourself a cup of something warm and wonderful, and page through our projects. Before you know it, seeds of delightful gift ideas will begin sprouting, and soon, souls will be blossoming with happiness. A harvest rich indeed!

Table of Contents

The materials you carefully choose for your projects, including buttons bold and bright, can reflect a girl-friend's favorite color or personality.

Getting Started

Just about everything you need for the projects throughout this book can be found at your local craft or hobby store. Specialty items, such as sterling silver earring hooks and clasps or specific beads, are available at bead shops. The Internet also is a viable source for things such as purse handles, specialty beads, and vintage images and postcards.

Scrapbooking supplies have opened a whole new creative side to designing gifts from the heart. Embellishments such as borders, die cuts, lettering, patterned papers, photo corners, stamp sets, stencils, and stickers help dress up items such as candles, journals, and scrapbooks.

A sheet of floral paper becomes a very pretty card with decorative edge scissors, trim, and eyelets, while fabric and buttons help create a thoughtful gift tag.

Calligraphy kits are readily available at bookstores, craft stores, and through the Internet. With some practice, you can achieve distinct scrolls and lettering to personalize just about any project.

Everyday items such as an old soup can, yogurt container, and canning jar make a wonderful base for beautiful projects. So get ready to look beyond the ordinary and create something wonderful that's from the heart and made with your own hands.

Tips and Techniques

CALLIGRAPHY

Hand lettering makes a beautiful addition to just about any project. We used it for our recipe book, cake box, and soap wrap projects. If you're just beginning, a calligraphy kit is a great way to get started. Before you write on any creation, you will want to practice on a scrap sheet of paper until you get the lettering just right. Then cut out the word, phrase, or paragraph and place it directly above where you want to write. It will serve as a great guide for both the centering and spacing of your letters. You may also want to consider your computer as a viable alternative. With hundreds of unique fonts available for purchase on the Internet and at office supply stores, you can replicate the elegant presentation of calligraphy. Vellum is a wonderful paper to use when printing your lettering; just be sure that your selection is printable or else the ink may smudge. Also keep in mind that the better your computer printer, the finer the printing.

COLLAGE

Collage is all about seeing the extraordinary in the ordinary. It is taking tiny pieces to make an exquisite new whole. The first step to creating interesting collages is to open your eyes to the realms of possibility. Once you've determined what it is you want to create, then comes the fun of choosing just the right elements—everything from notebook paper to vintage papers, photographs, and fabrics are fair game. We simply use white glue mixed

with water to tack everything down. We've used collage to make our candy jar, garland, sugar cookie box, and even to make the iron-on transfer for our pillow. The final product is actually a color copy of our collage, so there's no need for a sealer.

DECOUPAGE

Decoupage takes scraps of paper and turns them into something beautiful. Use decoupage when you want to create a three-dimensional effect or when you want all the pieces sealed in place. We've used decoupage to create an old-fashioned picture frame. By covering the surface of each torn piece of newsprint with either glue or a decoupage medium, we covered the surface curves smoothly. Just be sure to smooth each individual piece as you go so there are no air bubbles underneath. If you do use a sealer, look for one with a matte finish so it doesn't spoil the look of vintage papers.

GIFT WRAPPING

Many people spend a great deal of time thinking of just the right gift, and then wait until the very last moment to wrap it. Since first impressions count, we've come up with several fabulous wraps that let you get creative with paint, vintage fabrics, silk flowers, ribbon, double-sided tape, and a glue gun. So whether your gift is something small or large, our ideas will turn even a plain box into a work of art she'll treasure.

LABEL MAKING

A handmade label is a quick way to add a thoughtful touch to any package. We love vintage manila tags, but if you can't find them, make your own by adding round reinforcements and tea-staining new ones. To give any label vintage charm, tear the edges of a thick paper. When perfection matters, use a scrapbooking deco cutter as your guide. Then use anything from lettering to charms and stickers to decorate your label with personal flair.

LAMINATING

Laminating used to be a job that everyone outsourced, but today, home laminating machines are readily available at most craft stores. We used ours to make our bookmark, but they would also be wonderful for laminating recipe cards or children's artwork to create one-of-a kind gifts like placemats or game boards. Many laminating machines even come with an adhesive cartridge, so they are also great for scrapbooking, or anytime you've got a sticky project in the works!

LETTER APPLICATIONS

If hand lettering isn't your gift, no need to despair. Any number of options await, from rub-on letters to stamps, stickers, and even computer-generated sentiments. For those eager to try something new, embossing also creates an elegant effect. Simply print your message on vellum paper, then sprinkle with embossing powder while the ink is still wet. Then emboss with heat gun. We've used letter applications to embellish everything from a clipboard to handmade labels.

PHOTOCOPYING

With the advent of the photocopier, the wide world of

pattern and color became readily available for art. We've copied everything from burlap and vintage floral cloths to candies, antique letters, pages of books, and even watch parts for use in our collages. Try reducing or enlarging your images, then use them in unexpected ways. Or print out a copy in one color. We've cut out puffy clouds from an antique letter copied in blue, and made flowers from one copied in pink. Photocopying is ideal for any project involving collage or decoupage. We invite you to copy the images and patterns provided throughout this book, or dare to dream up some of your own. And when it comes to using your treasured photographs, be sure to use a copier so that you may preserve the original.

SCRAPBOOKING

Scrapbooking has become a national pastime, but many women still don't realize its full gift-giving potential. We've used the same stickers, stamps, and embellishments that make scrapbook pages come to life to decorate other objects including a clipboard, journal, and a bookmark. Or for a gift that's both personal and practical, instead of giving a blank scrapbook, we love the idea of creating a custom cover specific to the special event she's celebrating —or perhaps even simply in honor of your friendship. Then let her have the fun of filling in the pages.

SIMPLE BEADING

Never has jewelry making been so accessible. Craft and jewelry wire, pliers, beads, stones, and clasps are all readily available at craft stores, and many of these stores even teach classes for those who want to learn the basics. We love all the usual gift ideas—including necklaces, bracelets, and earrings, but also think key chains and even eyeglass chains can be fun and funky variations.

Feel Good Sugar Cookies

2/3 c. shortening
3/4 c. sugar
1 tsp. vanilla
1 egg
4 tsp. milk
2 c. all-purpose flour
1 1/2 tsp. baking powder
1/4 tsp. salt

CHAPTER ONE

Lifting the Spirits

"It's the friends you can call at 4 a.m. that matter." —Marlene Dietrich

There are those friends we can count on for coffee or a laugh, but the good ones are the ones we call, and who call us, when spirits are low. For those true friends who have gabbed and giggled, wept and rejoiced with us, we offer gift ideas meant to brighten her days and let her know she's loved.

It's so easy to take our best friends for granted, especially when the demands of home and family press in close. So why not make a relaxed moment all the more enjoyable by spending it fashioning something fun and completely impractical for the friend who has always seen you through.

If you can't wait, by all means, deliver it straight away. But if you're one for surprises, wait until the day when her hard drive has crashed, losing scads of hours of work, or her husband has left for a golfing weekend after which the kids all promptly came down with the flu. After all, these are the days when we most savor a favor.

An unexpected gift might just give her the license she needs to open a box of bon bons and get lost in a good book, or put in a video for the children and enjoy a long, solitary soak in a fragrant tub. Sometimes it takes a friend to encourage us to indulge ourselves.

Feel Good Sugar Cookies Box & Recipe Card

MATERIALS

- 1" craft brush
- Decoupage glue
- Ribbon
- Scissors
- Tissue paper
- White fold-up box

INSTRUCTIONS

Color photocopy elements (pages 18-19); cut out. Assemble box and decoupage elements in place with craft brush. Write your favorite recipe for sugar cookies on recipe card provided.

Bake small batch of sugar cookies (see sample recipe, below); set aside to cool completely.

Tuck tissue paper inside box; add cookies to fill. Embellish with big bow or two and tuck in your recipe card.

INGREDIENTS

- 1 cup butter, softened
- 1 ½ cups white sugar
- 2 eggs
- 1 teaspoon vanilla extract
- 2 tablespoons milk
- 2 cups all-purpose flour
- 1 teaspoon baking powder
- ½ teaspoon salt

Sugar Cookies Recipe

DIRECTIONS

1. In large bowl, cream together butter and sugar until fluffy. Beat in eggs one at a time, then stir in vanilla extract and milk. In separate bowl, combine flour, baking powder, and salt; gradually blend into creamed mixture to form soft dough. Cover or wrap dough and refrigerate overnight.

2. Preheat oven to 400 degrees. Lightly grease cookie sheets.

3. Roll out half of dough at a time on lightly floured surface. Keep remaining dough refrigerated. Roll until about ¼" thick.

4. Place cookies ½" apart on cookie sheets.

5. Bake for 10 minutes in preheated oven, or until lightly browned. Cool on wire racks.

The see-through box front gives the receiver a peek into what awaits inside.

"FOR WHAT DO WE LIVE FOR, IF IT IS NOT TO MAKE LIFE LESS DIFFICULT FOR EACH OTHER?"
—GEORGE ELIOT

RECIPE CARD

BOX SIDES – ENLARGE TO FIT BOX

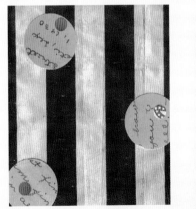

BOX FRONT AND BACK – ENLARGE TO FIT BOX

Very Relaxed Bath Salts

MATERIALS

- ½" silk ribbon
- 1" organdy ribbon
- Awl or sharp pencil
- Bath salts
- Clear liquid glue
- Dimensional foam stickers
- Drill and ¼" bit
- Embossing powder and heat gun
- Hot glue gun
- Paint can, small
- Purple patterned paper
- Scissors, sharp
- Sheet of vellum
- Silk flower, small
- Two sheets of coordinating patterned paper
- Wooden spoon, small

INSTRUCTIONS

Carefully drill small hole in top center of can.

Cut one circle from each patterned paper, one ¼" larger than other, to fit lid. Glue down. Using awl or sharp pencil, punch paper through drilled hole.

Cut floral patterned paper to fit side of can; adhere with clear liquid glue. Tear piece of purple patterned paper to fit center of can. Adhere to front of can with clear liquid glue.

Type in words "Bath Salts to soothe your Soul" on computer. Print on vellum paper. Before ink dries, sprinkle embossing powder onto words; tap off excess and emboss with heat gun.

Using scissors, cut words out and glue to can using clear liquid glue. Attach organdy ribbon with glue gun, placing dimensional foam sticker where ribbon ends at bottom of can.

Attach another dimensional foam sticker to label. Thread organdy ribbon through hole in top of can and back down. Secure by tying knot at top and bottom of lid.

Thread second organdy ribbon in top of can; tie into bow.

Attach silk flower to ribbon with glue gun. Tie sticker to organdy ribbon using silk ribbon. Thread silk ribbon through wooden spoon and tie to large organdy bow at top of can. Fill with bath salts.

(Left) A small wooden scoop is the perfect way to sprinkle bath salts into water.

A long soak helps wash away the worries of the day. A few simple bath essentials including salts, lotion, and bath slippers encourage a soothing retreat.

Bath Salts to soothe your Soul

PRECIOUS ARE ALL THINGS THAT COME FROM FRIENDS

PURE O

VIOLE

Memories of Mom Jar

MATERIALS

- Beads and buttons, various sizes
- Charm bracelet
- Computer and printer
- Decorative papers
- Decorative trim
- Drill and ⅛" bit
- Foam brush
- Gold cording, thin
- Hand-dyed silk ribbon
- Hot glue gun
- Liquid Laminate
- Mica flakes
- Printable vellum
- Strong-hold instant glue
- Tall glass jar with lid

INSTRUCTIONS

Print favorite sentiment and photo onto piece of vellum sized to full height and ⅓ circumference of jar.

Apply image to outside back of jar with foam brush and Liquid Laminate; let dry.

Cover vellum with piece of decorative paper applied same way. Finish edges with decorative trim applied with hot glue gun.

Drill ⅛" holes in lid of jar. String beads, buttons, small photos, and other memorabilia onto gold cording; create four or five strings of varying lengths, which will be suspended inside jar. Insert strings through holes in lid and tie knot to keep from pulling through.

Adhere decorative paper to lid of jar with foam brush and Liquid Laminate. Apply trim to edges of lid with hot glue gun.

Adhere two large beads atop each other with strong-hold instant glue; glue to top of lid. Sprinkle mica flakes in bottom of jar before placing lid on top of jar. Affix charm bracelet to rim of jar with hand-dyed silk ribbon.

Many times, mom becomes a treasured friend sometimes lost too soon. Here an everyday jar with lid becomes a tribute to a loved one embellished with fond remembrances: a photo of mom at a young age, prayer beads, and the hospital band she wore when her daughter was born.

(Right) The rich combination of silk ribbon, beads, charms, and textured fabric makes this jar pretty from all angles.

(Bottom right) Each of the strings and ribbon are held in place by drilling small holes at the top of the lid and threading through the strings, which are then kept in place with simple knots. It's hidden by decorative paper glued over the lid.

Girl Talk

Upon hearing that a dear friend had lost her mother, one close friend ordered a dozen of her favorite roses and had them sent to her house. The card read: "These roses remind me of the many blessings you have given. Your mother left many legacies— you by far are the greatest."

A childhood photograph is photocopied, cut out with decorative edge scissors, and framed beautifully with a glitter edge.

25

Lavender Sachet Basket

MATERIALS

- ¼" hole punch
- 1" craft brush
- 1"-wide ribbon
- 6-8 oz. yogurt container
- Cardstock
- Decorative edge scissors
- Decoupage glue
- Scissors
- Streamer roll of crepe paper, pink
- Streamer roll of crepe paper, yellow
- Toothpick
- Two pipe cleaners
- White craft glue

INSTRUCTIONS

Color photocopy all paper elements (page 29).

Clean and dry yogurt container. Punch hole in each side.

Twist two pipe cleaners together to form one sturdy one. Feed through one side of yogurt container about 1" and twist closed. Form arch; feed through second side and twist closed.

To cover handle, glue crepe paper over handle and hole, and wrap crepe paper around and around until you come down to other side. Glue down over handle and hole on this side as well.

Cover yogurt container by gluing edge of crepe streamer down inside bottom of cup. Bring streamer up and down outside, give it a twist underneath and dab with white glue; go up opposite side, then down inside again. Use dab of glue here as well. Repeat this as many times as necessary to completely cover container.

Cut out about 25 basket trim pieces. To form these, cut 6" strips of crepe streamer, cutting points on top and bottom, and twisting once in center.

Glue these vertically all around basket with dab of glue only on twisted center area so top and bottom edges are loose.

Wrap with ribbon and tie off at back of basket.

Cut out ribbon trim with decorative edge scissors, glue end to end to form one long 12" strip and glue on top of ribbon.

Cut out face and pink roses garland elements and decoupage to cardstock; set aside to dry, then cut out.

Cut out approximately 40 yellow flower petals from crepe paper. Starting at rounded edge, roll each petal around toothpick. Loosen a bit when you get to base of petal to release toothpick. Slide it out, leaving petal in tight roll while you do all the rest. This sets curl. Set aside.

(Continued on page 28)

A sweet face surrounded by paper petals sends a message of goodwill. The handle makes it easy to hang the basket just about anywhere, or, simply set the basket on a shelf.

(Right) Some say that just looking at a lavender plant can make you feel better. This favorite herb is the perfect aromatic mate to this sweet basket.

(Continued from page 26)

Cut out 2 ½" diameter circle out of cardstock. Unfurl petals and begin gluing around perimeter in layers until you reach center. Using curls pattern, cut four 4" pieces out of book print.

Cut strips (like eye lashes) of book print element, leaving ¼"-wide edge along top to hold curl strip together. With edge of scissors, gently curl book print up.

Glue these pieces around face from underneath, glue pink roses garland behind crepe floret and face to center, then glue entire piece to front of basket.

PINK ROSES GARLAND

BOOK PRINT

FACE

PETAL

BASKET TRIM

RIBBON TRIM

Bon Bons Candy Container

MATERIALS

- 1" craft brush
- 8 ½" glass canning jar
- Decorative edge scissors
- Decoupage glue
- Ribbon
- Scissors

INSTRUCTIONS

Wash canning jar thoroughly; let dry.

Color photocopy label element (page 33); cut out. Brush back of label with light coat of decoupage glue and apply to glass jar; let dry.

Finish jar by tying pretty ribbon around its rim; fill with your choice of candies.

Girl Talk

A group of college friends gathered once to help one of their own get over a failed relationship. They each packed a bag of assorted treats and headed to the guest of honor's home, where they, dressed in black, staged a memorial service of sorts. On the menu was chicken soup for her soul, a tombstone cake, and a well-scripted eulogy. They laughed, they cried, and together they remembered the old adage, "If you love something, set it free..."

Lean on Me

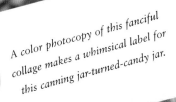

A color photocopy of this fanciful collage makes a whimsical label for this canning jar-turned-candy jar.

"FOR THERE IS NO FRIEND LIKE A SISTER IN CALM OR STORMY WEATHER; TO CHEER ONE ON
THE TEDIOUS WAY, TO FETCH ONE IF ONE GOES ASTRAY, TO LIFT ONE IF ONE TOTTERS DOWN,
TO STRENGTHEN WHILST ONE STANDS." —CHRISTINA ROSSETTI

(Right) Pastel-colored meringues are a pretty choice for this candy jar. Feel free to fill your jar with candy sugar sticks, chocolate truffles, or any other favorite treat.

Meringue Cookies

INGREDIENTS

- ½ cup chopped walnuts or slivered almonds; optional
- ½ teaspoon lemon juice
- 1 cup sugar
- 3 egg whites at room temperature

DIRECTIONS

1. Beat egg whites until stiff, but not dry. Add sugar gradually, while continuing to beat, two tablespoons at a time.

2. Continue beating until mixture holds shape. Fold in nuts, then add lemon juice.

3. Line baking sheet with wax paper. Drop by teaspoonfuls onto wax paper.

4. Bake at 275 degrees for approximately ½ hour or until dry but not hard. Cool completely.

5. Store in cookie jar or container to keep fresh.

Healing Keychain

MATERIALS

- 18-25 assorted stone chips
- Craft wire, .15 diameter
- Key ring
- Round-nose pliers
- Rounding tool
- Side-cutting pliers
- Three earring pins
- Two pewter spiritual beads

INSTRUCTIONS

Divide 27" strand of craft wire into three 9" pieces; cut with side-cutting pliers. Use round-nose pliers to curl one end of each piece of wire. Combine all three pieces and slide on pewter bead over all three strands.

Separate one piece of wire from bunch and make one curl with rounding tool. Slide stone chip over that piece of wire. Make another curl going in opposite direction; slide over another stone chip.

Continue rotating curls and chips on all three strands until you achieve desired length. Combine three pieces of wire and once again slide pewter bead over, combining strands into one again. Push bead down as tight as possible, then make large loop and wrap remaining wire around base of loop.

To make dangles, pick up earring pins and slide three chips on each pin. Pick up first earring pin (with all three chips on it) and make small loop at end with pliers. Slide this loop through one of circle curls at end of key chain. Once it has slid through, wrap remainder of pin around to close it off.

Continue doing this with other pins. Add key ring to finish.

Expert Tip

Some thoughtful sentiments of metaphysical stones include:

Aventurine: Enhances creativity and brings prosperity. Diffuses negativity; balances male-female energy.

Carnelian: Grounds and anchors one in the present surroundings; motivates success in business and aids positive life choices.

Citrine: Stone of prosperity; attracts wealth and success; brings happiness and generosity.

Garnet: Energizes and revitalizes, balances energy, brings serenity.

Jasper: Supreme nurturer; brings tranquility and wholeness, protection, and grounding.

Moonstone: Stone of new beginnings; connected to the moon and intuition; soothes and calms emotions.

Rose Quartz: Stone of unconditional love; brings about deep inner healing; encourages self-forgiveness and acceptance.

Tourmaline: Synthesizes love and spirituality; promotes inner peace.

Choose stones with metaphysical qualities and include a dangling charm that reads "hope," "love," or "believe" to silently send a message of strength.

A heart is the symbol of love,
shared between man and woman,
woman and child, and friends
both old and new.

CHAPTER TWO

When She Falls in Love

"Where there is great love there are always miracles." —Willa Cather

The rustle of silk and a misty veil, little pink toes, and first coos and smiles—life's most magical moments may be short-lived, but they remain etched in our memories forever. Perhaps that's why some of our all-time favorite gifts are the ones that bring these memories flooding back.

Whether it's a baby on the way or the wedding of a lifetime, the projects we've created here are meant to help our girlfriends celebrate—and commemorate—the loves of their lives. And after all, who better to champion new love than the friends with whom we've gabbed about wedding gowns and baby names for years?

Maybe you've listened to her tragic tales of dates gone bad, and were as thrilled as she was when she finally found Mr. Right. Or maybe you've experienced every step of her pregnancy vicariously—and now know more than you ever dreamed possible about everything from maternity fashions to the hottest nursery hues.

Now that the time has come to celebrate her dreams come true, what better way to share in the thrill than with a gift that comes straight from your heart to hers? Whether you're planning a shower, or simply searching for just the right gift, we've selected projects she'll be sure to treasure.

Baby Blanket

MATERIALS

- 1 ½ yards ducky fabric
- 1 ½ yards yellow plaid fabric
- Computer
- Five sheets iron-on transfer paper
- Iron
- Photo editing software or printer fabric
- Photographs
- Pins
- Scissors
- Sewing machine
- Skein of pink/white eyelash yarn
- Skein of yellow eyelash yarn

INSTRUCTIONS

Wash and dry fabric. Cut both fabrics to 31" x 36".

Using remaining fabric, cut four 5 ¼" squares and one 7" square of yellow plaid fabric. From ducky fabric, cut one 6 ½" square; set aside.

Using photo editing software program, edit chosen photos for blanket, adding text and other desired patterns, or simply print photo on printer fabric following directions on package.

To assemble quilt, iron main photo to ducky fabric. Place large yellow square directly in center, then pin ducky fabric on top.

Using decorative stitch, sew photo and fabrics to quilt. Iron remaining photos to smaller yellow squares; sew to quilt, one in each corner.

Clip yellow squares ¼" apart to seams. Place two fabric panels right sides together and sew, leaving 4" space for turning. Turn right side out; iron seams so they lay flat, especially space for turning.

Sew yarn to edge of quilt by holding strands of yarn in one hand, and sewing yarn down with other. Another way to do this is to use special foot on sewing machine to "couch" threads to quilt; or have quilt shop hem stitch quilt, then blanket stitch around. Wash quilt to fray squares.

Expert Tip
. . . .
The idea of a memory quilt is to use pictures as a special keepsake for both baby and mom. Photos may include baby pictures of mother and father and nursery characters.

My squeaky

Duckie

Rub a dub dub,

What do I need in my tub?

Welcome a little one with a blanket just as soft and sweet as the little toes and fingers that will be warmed by it.

39

Friendship Hearts Garland

MATERIALS

- 1" craft brush
- Awl
- Crepe paper streamer
- Decorative edge scissors
- Decoupage glue
- Five 4" x 4" papier-mâché heart ornaments (available at craft stores)
- Hot glue gun
- Needle-nose pliers
- Scissors
- Six yards of silk ribbon
- White craft glue
- Wire cutters
- Wire hangers

INSTRUCTIONS

Remove gold hanging strings from ornaments. Color photocopy all elements (pages 43-45); cut out. Cut out edge trim elements with decorative edge scissors.

Glue two 6" pieces together to form 12" long strips of edge trim; glue on heart edges.

Decoupage hearts to papier-mâché ornaments, one front, one back.

Cut two 2-yard-long strips of ribbon and six 3" pieces of ribbon. Make "needle" to feed ribbon through hearts by cutting 6" piece of wire hanger. Straighten it out, bend closed ¼" loop in end.

Using awl, punch two holes on each side about 2" apart.

String one 2-yard-long ribbon through top holes, then second one through bottom holes.

Cinch up ends and in between hearts by tying with 3" pieces of ribbon. Add little bows here and there where you like.

To make crepe paper berry balls, tear crepe paper streamer into 8" lengths, run thin line of white glue down center of streamer strip, and roll in palm of your hands firmly until it forms small ball.

Set aside to dry and glue on to ribbons randomly to finish your garland.

Throughout the years

40

Spread thoughts of love with a garland embellished with images provided, or you may choose to use your own. Consider photos of friends or other loved ones.

"INTIMATE RELATIONSHIPS CANNOT SUBSTITUTE FOR A LIFE PLAN. BUT TO HAVE ANY MEANING OR VIABILITY AT ALL, A LIFE PLAN MUST INCLUDE INTIMATE RELATIONSHIPS."
—HARRIET LERNER

(Right) The backs of the papier-mâché heart ornaments are finished off with photocopied pages from old books and turn-of-the-century postcards hand-colored in select areas.

Girl Talk

A soon-to-be bride spent her bachelorette weekend with a group of her best girlfriends— some from high school and college and others met in between and after. As they primped before heading out for dinner, each friend walked into the powder room, where the bachelorette was getting ready, to ask a simple question. One by one, each friend was met with a bellyaching laugh when the guest of honor noticed their tops—T-shirts with the bachelorette's photo, her third-grade class picture and dancing at homecoming among them. After the parade of images, the bachelorette headed out for the evening with pictures of her past not far behind.

EMBELLISHMENT

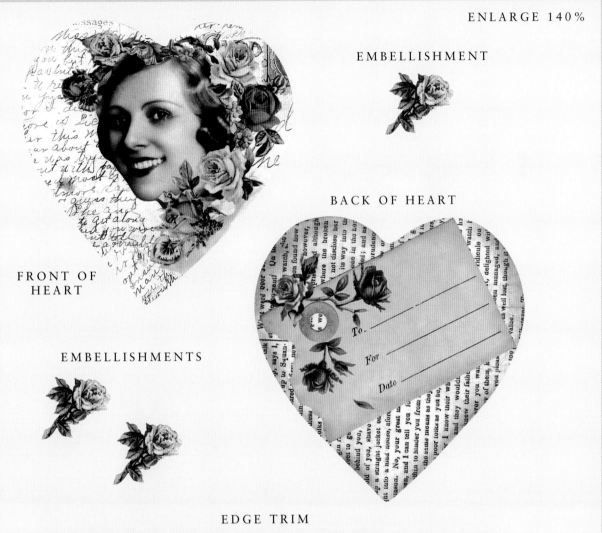

FRONT OF
HEART

BACK OF HEART

EMBELLISHMENTS

EDGE TRIM

ENLARGE 166%

FRONTS OF HEARTS

EDGE TRIM

ENLARGE 166%

BACKS OF HEARTS

EDGE TRIM

Kindred Spirits Scrapbook Cover

MATERIALS

- 1 ½" green organza ribbon
- Craft paper
- Double-sided tape
- Favorite photo
- Foam dimensional stickers
- Orange fiber
- Rub-on words
- Scrapbook with photo frame
- Seed beads

INSTRUCTIONS

Adhere double-sided tape around scrapbook's photo placement.

Place album over large sheet of craft paper. Peel second side of tape and sprinkle beads over tape.

Tip album to remove excess beads. Collect on paper and return excess to bead container for reuse.

Rub on words following package directions.

Tie green ribbon into bow near spine. Tie orange fiber through tag dimensional sticker and attach to bow. Attach remaining stickers to album.

Girl Talk

. . . .

A dear friend was an avid scrapbooker long before anyone thought about archival quality or acid-free papers. Every pep rally and swim meet were documented, amid newsprint album pages that included dried petals from formal dance corsages. She passed along the bug, and soon the two friends had shelves of bulging memory albums. All these years later, they continue to fill the pages of scrapbooks and use the time they work on them to count their blessings. While books of today showcase the growth of their children, and reflect the art form scrapbooking has become, the fading photos of the tall, skinny blonde and the short, smiling brunette are treasured documentation of kindred spirits that bonded long ago while pasting keepsakes in an album.

Chronicle a lifetime of memories with a Kindred Spirits scrapbook, a wonderful gift for a girlfriend just falling in love.

Let's Celebrate! Flower Cone

MATERIALS

- ½" satin or silk ribbon
- 8 ½" x 11" decorative paper
- Circle hole punch
- Decorative edge scissors
- Embellishments
- Paper towel
- Rubber band, plastic sandwich bag, twist tie
- Scissors
- Stapler or hot glue gun

INSTRUCTIONS

Clip edges of paper with decorative edge scissors. Roll paper into cone. Staple or hot glue paper together at what would be front of cone.

Punch small hole on each side of cone, or at back, and pull ribbon through holes, securing each side with knot. Leave enough ribbon for cone to hang freely.

Gather freshly cut flowers in bunch, wrap wet paper towel around base of stems, and secure with rubber band. Place flowers in plastic bag; tie bag closed with twist tie. Place flowers in cone.

Embellish front of flower cone to your heart's content! Consider ribbons, artificial flowers, silk leaves, and beads.

Girl Talk

Now married, a dear friend still keeps a handful of mementos from her wedding day. Among the fond memories leading up to this special day are the Friday nights she shared with her best friends, crafting wedding decorations including flower cones. Her friends thought she was crazy, making all of the party favors and decorations, but they were more than happy to lend a hand.

48

Paper cones lend an air of festivity
in honor of a bride-to-be or any other
friend celebrating a special occasion.

Indulge in time just for the girls with
a fun crafting party. All you need are
a few supplies and one of the simple
project ideas featured in this chapter.

CHAPTER THREE

Girls Night In

*"Some people go to priests, others to poetry;
I to my friends." –Virginia Woolf*

Remember sleepovers…munching on popcorn, talking until dawn, and trying out new makeup and hairstyles? "Girls Night In" is the grown-up version, where everyone gets to dish and munch. But instead of getting glamorous, everyone fashions a fun craft and leaves at a reasonable hour!

After you've gathered a friend or two—or more—all you need is a craft you can complete in an evening. This chapter features a collection of favorites, all uncomplicated enough to ensure that the conversation is hopping even as hands are flying. All of the supplies necessary can easily be found at your local craft store, and the projects don't require an artist's degree.

Some girlfriends enjoy staying in so much that they meet regularly—each taking turns gathering supplies and bringing snacks. For the holidays one year, some even plan a marathon night, where cookies are baked or gifts are made for friends, teachers, and family.

And through it all we're able to connect, swap stories, and tell jokes that make us laugh until we cry.

Forget-Me-Not Eyeglasses Chain

MATERIALS

- Bent-nose pliers
- Craft wire, 0.18" diameter
- One package of crystals, bronze
- One strand of Garnet barrels
- One strand of seed beads
- Two crimp beads
- Two to three strands of Tourmaline ovals
- Wire cutters

INSTRUCTIONS

Cut craft wire to desired length, about 40". Slide on just enough seed beads to make circle to fit ends of glasses.

Finish circle by sliding on crimp bead and crimp tight with pliers to secure. Begin beading with this pattern: 1 Garnet barrel, 10 Tourmaline ovals, 1 Garnet barrel, 1 crystal, 1 Garnet barrel, 10 Tourmaline ovals.

Continue this pattern to desired length. Finish ends with seed beads to match reverse side. Add crimp bead and tightly close with pliers to finish.

Expert Tip

When picking out crimp beads, it is helpful to use sterling silver. They are easier to secure and hold better. If you use bent-nose pliers, it is best to fasten the crimp bead on the end that is beaded. The bent design has a smaller tip and allows you to get into tight places, to be sure that the crimp bead will not slip.

Whether your girlfriends wear eyeglasses or sunglasses, they'll love stringing their favorite beads to make this eyeglasses chain.

Those Who Matter Journal

INSTRUCTIONS

Cut two pansies from patterned paper. Glue to journal at right side. Tear strip of patterned paper and glue onto journal, slightly covering pansies as shown.

Cut two accents from vellum patterned paper and attach to journal using pop dots. Attach letter stickers, metal stickers, and metal tag stickers to journal.

Remove paper from tag so only frame remains and adhere to journal. Stamp word "journal" in frame, tie locket charm to frame using silk ribbon, and glue onto journal.

Tie remaining heart charm to elastic closure using piece of fiber. Finish journal by tying various fibers to spine.

Girl Talk

. . . .

A woman once walked into a crowded party alone. Looking around, she spotted no familiar faces. Then a great friend popped in unexpectedly— instantly the night was filled with laughter. How often our friends are the life rafts that save us from a certain disaster!

MY GIRL FRIENDS

journal

secret

Simple embellishments turn a plain journal into a worthy volume of your favorite treasured photos. All you need are some basic scrapbooking supplies and adhesives.

Bookmark Smart

MATERIALS

- Buttons, various colors and sizes
- Circle hole punch
- Fibers and ribbon
- Green cardstock
- Laminating machine
- Paper trimmer
- Patterned paper
- Scissors
- Sewing machine and thread
- Stickers
- Temporary adhesive

INSTRUCTIONS

Cut green cardstock to desired size using paper trimmer; cut patterned paper half its width. Attach patterned paper directly to center using temporary adhesive.

Sew each side of patterned paper to green cardstock with decorative stitch; attach stickers as desired. Laminate bookmark; trim around edges, leaving scant border of laminate.

Create hole at top with hole punch and thread fibers and ribbon through hole. Thread desired buttons through ribbons and fibers.

Expert Tip

10 great books for book-smart girlfriends:

"Bel Encanto" *by Ann Patchett*

"Divine Secrets of the Ya-Ya Sisterhood" *by Rebecca Wells*

"Girlfriends Forever" *by Susan Branch*

"Little Women" *by Louisa May Alcott*

"Memoirs of a Geisha" *by Arthur Golden*

"Red Tent" *by Anita Diamant*

"Saving Graces" *by Patricia Gaffney*

"The Secret Life of Bees" *by Sue Monk Kidd*

"Sense and Sensibility" *by Jane Austen*

"A Woman of Independent Means" *by Elizabeth Forsythe Hailey*

By using a simple laminating kit, this festive bookmark is made to last a lifetime. Consider buttons, beads, stickers, and other embellishments that reflect your friend's hobbies or interests.

A friend is the loving GARDENER who inspires the soul to blossom

Recipe Booklet

MATERIALS

- ¼" hole punch
- ¼" posts
- 4 ¼" x 6" cards, 10-20
- Bone folder
- Cardstock, assorted colors
- Exacto knife
- Glue stick
- Metal or straight-edge ruler
- Pencil
- Plain or decorative heavyweight paper
- Scissors
- Scrap paper

INSTRUCTIONS

Cut cardstock to 4 ¼" x 6" to create recipe cards.

Make template for hole punching recipe pages (Diagram A, page 61). *Note:* Exact placement is critical.

Hole punch all recipe cards in lower left corner using template as guide (Diagram B). Hole should be about ¼" from bottom and ¼" from left side.

Use spine template to measure spine for cover (Diagram C). Stack recipe cards; use paper strip to measure and mark. Width of spine is determined by quantity of recipe cards.

Mark dimensions on heavyweight paper with pencil and cut cover. Score on all fold (dotted) lines with bone folder and ruler (Diagram D).

Using template, hole punch cover, both front and back (Diagram E). Glue inner flaps, front and back, along edge. Assemble recipe pages within cover with posts.

Decorate cover with your choice of watercolor art, scrapbooking embellishments, or even decoupaged assortment of food images.

(Above) Vary the colors of the recipe cards to complement the illustrations on the white cards. (Below) Plastic posts hold the cards in place.

One cannot think well, love well, sleep well, if one has not dined well. —VIRGINIA WOOLF

A culinary-themed watercolor personalizes this recipe booklet cover. However, you can create your own with scrapbooking embellishments or decoupage.

> "IN THE SWEETNESS OF FRIENDSHIP LET THERE BE LAUGHTER, AND SHARING OF PLEASURES. FOR IN THE DEW OF LITTLE THINGS THE HEART FINDS ITS MORNING AND IS REFRESHED."
> —KAHLIL GIBRAN

(Right) Rename recipes with a whimsical twist and create your own themed cards with light-hearted watercolors or colored pencil drawings.

Girl Talk

At wedding showers, it is often customary that guests bring an index card scrawled with their favorite recipe for the bride-to-be. Forty years later, every single woman in a group of childhood friends still has these recipes. Good recipes—like a savored friendship—survive time.

Jam Tarts
of the
Queen of Hea

out shortcrust pastry until
t ¼ inch thick.
a pastry cutter cut into
ds a little larger than the
ed tins in which they'll
oked.
each round into its tin.
a little jam on each
d.
de a thin layer of water
the jam, to prevent
rying out during
g.

6. Bake for 10 minutes until light browned, in a moderat hot oven at 425 degrees F.
7. To check if thoroughly cooked, lift a tart from the tin and look at its base.
8. Cool on a cake rack and keep under a close guard.

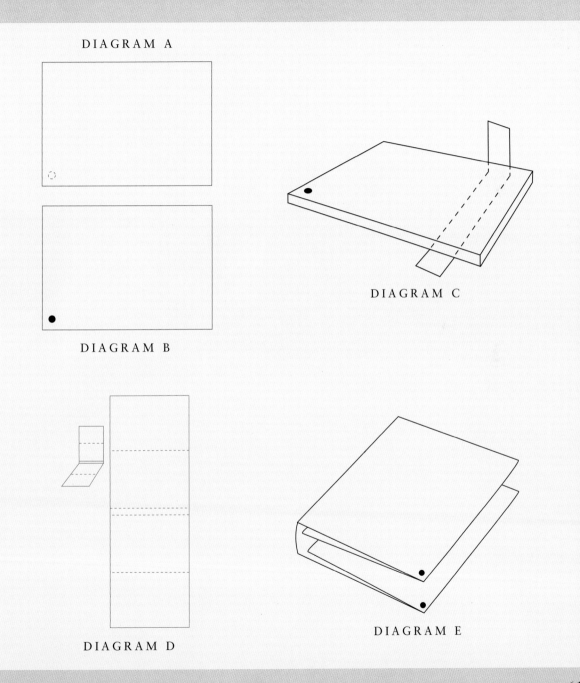

DIAGRAM A

DIAGRAM B

DIAGRAM C

DIAGRAM D

DIAGRAM E

61

Best friends are always so thoughtful! Celebrate a new home with a heartwarming gift.

CHAPTER FOUR

From the Heart, For the Home

*"Ah! There is nothing like staying at home,
for real comfort."* —Jane Austen

Finding a new house is a beginning in more ways than one. Whether your girlfriend has moved across the country, or simply across town, transforming blank walls and empty spaces into a home doesn't happen in one day—or even one week.

That's why we love these ideas for thought-filled house-warming gifts. They are just the kind of sentimental touches that will bring comfort to her soul—even if she still has stacks of boxes all over the house!

Great housewarming gifts don't have to be big or expensive. At a time like this, it's definitely the thought that counts. Something as small and simple as a fragrant soap, personalized with a decorative band, can make her feel special every time she washes her hands.

And since it takes time to establish new friends after she's moved, reminders of cherished friendships mean more now than ever. A handmade pillow for her bed or a candle for the table will help keep any lonely thoughts at bay, making her feel surrounded by love.

Remember, every thoughtful touch helps when she's transforming a new house into a home where comfort and contentment await.

Tin Can Fairy Light

MATERIALS

- 1" craft brush
- 3D foam dots
- 19-gauge wire
- Awl and drill
- Cardstock
- Crepe paper streamer, beige
- Crystal beads
- Decorative edge scissors
- Decoupage glue
- Hot glue gun
- Tin can (4 ½" tall x 3" diameter)
- Needle-nose pliers
- Needle and thread
- Tea light candle
- Wire cutters

INSTRUCTIONS

Cut 20" piece of wire with wire cutters. Color photocopy all paper elements (page 67).

With drill, make several ¼" holes in tin can. With awl, make two small holes (for handle) 4 ½" apart on sides of tin can (use tin can cover to align this, if needed).

Decoupage tin can cover, back seam cover (cut out this piece with decorative edge scissors) and Pixie to cardstock; set aside to dry, then cut out.

Wrap tin can cover around and hot glue in place; cover this seam with back seam cover element. Use doubled 3D dots on back of Pixie and attach to front of tin can.

With awl, punch holes through paper cover to coincide with holes in can.

To make crepe paper ruching, take running stitch down center of crepe paper streamer. Gather (do this delicately) and hot glue around top and bottom.

To create handle, make small loop in one end of wire, curl up a bit and thread beads on. Insert this through outside right handle hole. Continue up about 3", make a loop, insert bead, then make another loop. Make last loop and insert another bead.

Go down 3" again; go through left handle hole, insert beads, then make another curl.

Ready to hang just about anywhere, this Tin Can Fairy Light needs only a tea light candle tucked inside to cast a lovely glow.

A strip of aged paper cut with decorative edge scissors makes a wonderful finishing touch at the back of the can.

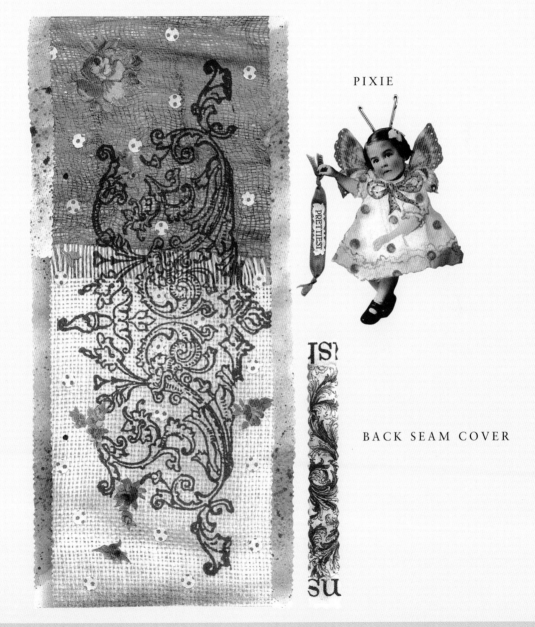

PIXIE

PRETTIEST

BACK SEAM COVER

Iron-On Transfer Pillow

MATERIALS

- Burlap, ivory
- Fabric glue
- Hot glue gun
- Iron and ironing board
- Iron-on transfer copy paper
- Muslin
- Pillow form, small
- Pompoms, pastel colors
- Rickrack
- Scissors
- Sewing machine
- Twine

INSTRUCTIONS

Cut 2 pieces of burlap about 5" larger than pillow. Create standard pillow cover by sewing 3 sides together, with wrong sides out. Turn cover right side out, and stitch remaining side together.

Following instructions on transfer copy paper package, create iron-on transfer with collage artwork (page 71). Reduce to preferred size and be sure to reverse image for text.

Here, transfer was done on piece of muslin then attached to burlap pillow cover with fabric glue. For clean look, fold edges under to form hem.

Glue rickrack to borders of collage. Make tiny bow out of twine and glue in place. Hot glue pompoms around pillow.

Note: Be sure to reverse image for text.

Girl Talk

When one friend gives a gift, the thought behind each gift is often deeper than face value. This is especially true when celebrating a new home. For example, she's given one friend a candle to bring peace and a glimmer of hope to her family in a time of turmoil. Another time, she selected two houseplants to signify that early family's growth and beauty.

Sweet Sentiments

"The future belongs to those who believe in the beauty of their dreams. —Eleanor Roosevelt" reads the quote on this easy-to-make pillow.

69

"IF WE WOULD BUILD ON A SURE FOUNDATION IN FRIENDSHIP, WE MUST LOVE FRIENDS FOR THEIR SAKE RATHER THAN FOR OUR OWN." —CHARLOTTE BRONTE

(Right) Pink rickrack beautifully frames this pillow. The message can be altered to a favorite quote about friendship, love, or life.

Expert Tip

While a quote makes a wonderful sentiment on a pillow, also consider an iron-on transfer of the following:

- Collage of images depicting hobbies, favorite pastimes

- Excerpt from a treasured letter or note

- Favorite photograph of you and your girlfriend

- Humorous postcard or greeting card

- Invitation from college graduation or wedding

- Memento from a trip, such as a railway pass or museum ticket

- Photograph of "some-day" destination

- Special memory written in calligraphy

The future belongs to those who believe in the beauty of their dreams
- Eleanor Roosevelt

Soap Band

MATERIALS

- Decorative papers
- Glue stick
- Raffia, ribbon, or colored string
- Soap bar
- Sprig of lavender, flower, or herbs

INSTRUCTIONS

Tear decorative papers into 3" x 9" and 1" x 9" strips for soap band; assemble sprig of lavender between layers then secure layers in place at back of soap with glue.

Cut 2" square out of preferred paper and fold into envelope.

Glue in place.

Cut out 1" x 1 ⅜" letter from preferred paper. Write note and fold in half.

Insert letter into envelope and attach back of envelope to soap band with glue.

(Above) Inscribe a special sentiment and tuck inside the miniature envelope.

Expert Tip

To make your own glycerine soap, you will need:

- ½ teaspoon natural oil
- 2 cups rubbing alcohol
- 3 pounds of soap shavings
- 10 oz. sugar, moistened in just enough hot water to dissolve it, but as little water as possible
- 10 oz. vegetable glycerine

To make: Add soap shavings, glycerine, and ½ of alcohol to cold crock pot or double boiler. Add remaining alcohol very slowly. When pot is heated to 145 degrees, add other ingredients. Melt sugar in water in microwave, about 7 minutes. Add sugar to glycerine mixture; stir continuously until soap shavings are melted. When you get "strings," or rope-like ribbons falling off spoon you are using to mix, and little dropping off spoon hardens, you're done. Pour into soap mold or long form and cut when hardens.

Makes three pounds of soap.

A bar of soap becomes a messenger of good thoughts with a handmade paper band embellished with a sprig of lavender.

Angel Embellished Candle

MATERIALS

- Angel charm
- Brown tag
- Dotted ribbon
- Heat gun
- Hot glue gun
- Jute thread
- Letter stamps
- Mulberry tissue paper
- Padlock charm
- Pillar candle
- Postmark stamps
- Silk flowers
- Wax paper

INSTRUCTIONS

Tear mulberry paper into various sized strips and pieces (like you would to decoupage).

Attach pieces and strips to candle by heating section of candle with heat gun, allowing wax to melt.

Quickly and carefully attach mulberry pieces to candle by pressing paper into melted wax with wax paper. Wax should melt in small layer over top of paper. Continue until candle is covered as desired.

Randomly stamp postmark images and words onto candle. Attach ribbon to bottom of candle with hot glue gun. Tie and glue charm over knot.

Wrap jute around candle, like you're wrapping a gift. Tie jute at top of candle and hot glue flowers to embellish.

Stamp greeting on tag and glue angel below words. Attach tag with jute to top of candle. This candle is for decoration only. Remember, do not light!

(Above) Consider using a candle that smells heavenly for a gift that is pretty and fragrant. Since silk flowers have been adhered at top, this candle is for decorative purposes only.

LOVE

HOTEL
JUN
5

confide

Sparrow Pixie Refrigerator Magnet

MATERIALS

- 1" craft brush
- 3" x 4" papier-mâché ornament, rectangle
- 3D foam dots
- Crepe paper
- Decorative edge scissors
- Decoupage glue
- Glitter, copper
- Hot glue gun
- Magnet
- Scissors
- Thin silk ribbon
- White craft glue

INSTRUCTIONS

Remove gold string hanger from ornament. Color photocopy paper elements (page 79).

Cut out Sparrow Pixie element and decoupage to cardstock. Cut out all other elements and decoupage in place. Use decorative edge scissors on edge trim.

Glue trim end-to-end to form one long strip and glue in place. Glue thin piece of ribbon across back of Sparrow Pixie card area and add few extra glitter dots.

Attach Sparrow Pixie to piece with doubled 3D foam dots. Embellish glitter dots with extra copper glitter, and tie tiny bow with thin ribbon for Sparrow Pixie's necktie.

To make crepe paper berry balls, tear crepe paper streamer into 8" lengths. Run thin line of white glue down center of streamer strip and roll in palms of your hands firmly until it forms small ball; set aside to dry completely, then hot glue onto edge of magnet.

Glue magnet on back and leave yourself a note. "Lunch with Cathy on Wednesday!"

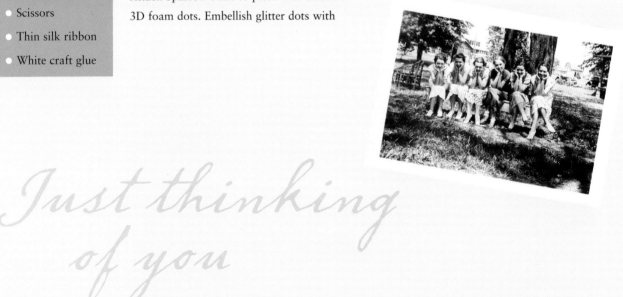

Just thinking of you

76

Welcome your friend home with a pretty magnet embellished with a special message delivered by Sparrow Pixie.

"CELEBRATE THE HAPPINESS THAT FRIENDS ARE ALWAYS GIVING, MAKE EVERY DAY A HOLIDAY AND CELEBRATE JUST LIVING!" —AMANDA BRADLEY

Adhered to the back are two long magnets that give the piece a more dimensional appearance.

FRONT OF MAGNET

Remember Molly Darling

Jim

Moravia N.Y. 1878

SPARROW PIXIE

Congratulations
Date 8-22-
What is best
that best I wish You
From

EDGE TRIM

BACK OF
MAGNET

To Fannie;—

May angels twine for t
a wreath of immortali
Your Friend,
Nellie May
Moravia Dec. 1st 1875

GLITTER DOTS

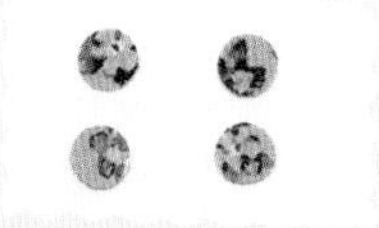

ENLARGE 156%

Grade-A Clipboard

MATERIALS

- Clipboard
- Decoupage glue
- Favorite image
- Foam brush
- Glue stick
- Hot glue gun
- Letter stamps
- Patterned paper
- Ribbon
- Round letter stickers
- School stickers
- Small letter stickers
- Twill word ribbon

INSTRUCTIONS

Attach alphabet-patterned paper to clipboard using foam brush and decoupage glue.

Tear gingham paper and decoupage over alphabet paper. Stamp words onto vintage image and decoupage onto clipboard. Place twill ribbon on far right side. Glue ends to back of clipboard with hot glue gun.

Repeat with black gingham ribbon on bottom of clipboard. Attach stickers as shown.

Tie various ribbons into knots and hot glue to top of clipboard, carefully placing next ribbon to cover knot. Attach alphabet-patterned paper to clipboard with glue stick. Embellish with stickers, ribbon, and favorite image.

(Left) Tying various ribbons at the top of the clipboard softens the look of the metal clip.

Whether she teaches lessons at home or at school, a clipboard decorated with stickers and ribbon makes a welcome gift.

A TeaCHeR hOLdS tHe fUtuRE iN hEr HANDs

DARCI

Presents big and small delight both the gift giver and the recipient of the thoughtful surprise tucked inside beautiful wrapping.

happy birthday to you friend

CHAPTER FIVE

Birthday Surprises

"She gives most who gives with joy." —Mother Teresa

Around the world, birthdays are celebrated with lovely traditions—from lighting candles in the window, to learning special dances, and even decorating the front door with pretty garlands. The common thread woven through every one of these international traditions is the joy that comes in giving something of ourselves. With this in mind, this year why not start some traditions all your own?

We love the idea of selecting one day a year to celebrate the lives of two or more of your finest friends. Throw a party where everyone's the guest of honor. Instead of heading off to the mall to buy your gifts, consider crafting something that expresses all that's unique and wonderful about your favorite girlfriends. For fun, you might pick names for gift giving, or have each person bring one gift for a grab bag.

We've gathered some of our favorite projects for birthday girls of all ages—from easy-to-make jewelry, to a purse that's fun to personalize with favorite colors, ribbons, and buttons.

If you're short on time, remember, making it personal doesn't have to mean laboring long. A handmade box—whether our clever cake box or our fabulous, feminine hatbox—turns any gift into a thoughtful treasure.

Of course, any birthday celebration wouldn't be complete without a cake, so on this one day, make it clear that all diets are off and by all means...Let Them Eat Cake!

Quartz Necklace & Earring Set

MATERIALS

- Bent-nose pliers
- Craft wire, 0.18 diameter
- Four Aztec Hilltribe beads
- Four Hilltribe "X" beads
- One lemon Quartz Faceted Nugget
- One strand of Champagne round pearls
- One strand of Citrine rectangles
- One strand of potato pearls, bronze
- Six crimp beads
- Ten Bali beads
- Toggle clasp
- Two earring hooks
- Two strands of potato pearls, mint green
- Wire cutters

INSTRUCTIONS

Necklace

Snip two strands of craft wire both 18" long with wire cutters. Loop wire through one end of toggle clasp; secure tightly with crimp bead. Cut excess beading wire, leaving two long strands to bead necklace onto.

Begin with 1 silver Bali bead and bead over both strands of wire. Separate strands and begin beading strand No. 1 with this pattern: 5 mint green pearls, 1 Citrine rectangle, 1 Hilltribe "X" bead, 3 mint green pearls, 1 bronze pearl, 1 round Champagne pearl, 3 Citrine rectangles, 2 mint green pearls, 1 Bali bead, 2 mint green pearls, 1 bronze pearl, 1 Aztec Hilltribe bead, 1 bronze pearl, 1 mint green pearl, 1 round Champagne pearl, 1 mint green pearl, 3 Citrine rectangles, 3 mint green pearls, 1 round Champagne pearl, 1 mint green pearl, 4 bronze pearls, 1 Bali bead.

Add Quartz Faceted Nugget. Mirror other half of necklace to match. When finished beading strand No. 1, put crimp bead on very end, leaving all slack to secure beads while you bead strand No. 2.

Begin strand No. 2 following this pattern: 15 mint green pearls, 1 Hilltribe "X" bead, 1 bronze pearl, 1 round Champagne pearl, 15 mint green pearls, 1 Aztec Hilltribe bead, 1 bronze pearl, 1 round Champagne pearl for center. Mirror other side to match.

Carefully cut secured crimp bead off of strand No. 1. Slide silver Bali bead over both strands, connecting them. Slide crimp bead over both strands and loop through remaining toggle. Feed wire back through crimp bead and crimp tight with pliers. Cut off excess wire to finish.

Your girlfriend will quickly fall in love with this two-tiered necklace and matching earring set, strung with a thoughtful selection of gems.

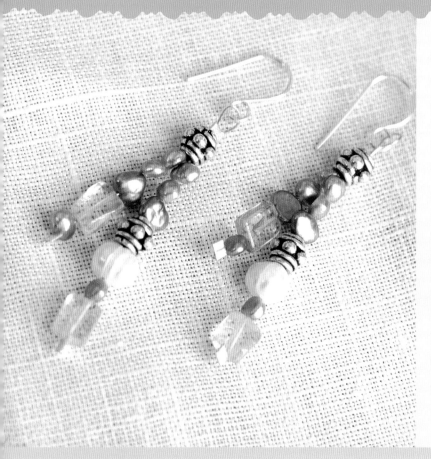

Earrings

Take 3" of craft wire and slide through attachment circle on earring hook. Bend wire in two and feed crimp bead over both ends. Slide crimp bead up to base of earring hook and secure tight.

Slide one Bali bead over both strands. Separate strands and begin beading strand No. 1 with 2 mint green pearls, 1 bronze pearl, 1 Citrine rectangle, 1 mint green pearl, and 1 crimp bead. Secure strand No. 1 tightly and cut off excess wire. Begin strand No. 2 with 2 mint green pearls, 1 bronze pearl, 1 Bali bead, 1 round Champagne pearl, 1 mint green pearl, and 1 Citrine rectangle.

Secure tightly with crimp bead and clip excess wire. Repeat with other earring to match.

Expert Tip

When beading multi-strand bracelets or necklaces, if you cut the wire long enough you can secure the first strand with a crimp bead at the very end. This will keep the beads from sliding off while you bead the other strands.

A sterling silver toggle is just the right clasp for this beautiful beaded necklace.

Not Just for Hats Box

MATERIALS

- Acrylic paint, white and green
- Drill and ½" bit
- Foam brush
- Glass beads (optional)
- Glass knob
- Hot glue gun
- Jute thread
- Metal charm
- Metal letters
- Papier-mâché hatbox
- Silk flowers
- Stencil tape
- Stylus or end of a paintbrush

INSTRUCTIONS

Paint entire box white; set aside to dry.

Mark evenly spaced stripes around box using stencil tape. (You also can do this with pencil and ruler, but pencil may leave indent in box.) Paint stripes green.

Using stylus or end of paintbrush, dot lid with green paint. Hot glue silk flowers around brim of hatbox, placing glass beads in center of flowers.

Drill or punch hole in center of lid, large enough to insert screw attached to glass knob. Insert knob; glue knob in place with hot glue gun.

Glue silk ribbon to lid around knob, gluing additional silk flowers to accent. Attach charm and metal letters to jute thread with hot glue gun. Tie to silk ribbon to complete.

(Left) Attach silk flowers to the rim of your box with a hot glue gun.

A papier-mâché hatbox is transformed into a decorative piece with a few craft items. Fill the box with baked goods, a hand-knitted scarf, or simply give by itself.

Ribbon Purse

MATERIALS

- ½"-wide black grosgrain ribbon, 27" long
- 16" black and white patterned ribbon (to attach letter buttons)
- Black canvas fabric, 22" wide x 11 ¼"
- Letter buttons
- Polka dot ribbon
- Ruler
- Seven different black and white ribbons in various widths, 22" long
- Sewing machine
- Sewing scissors
- Tan canvas fabric, 22" wide x 11 ¼"
- Temporary sewing adhesive or masking tape and pins
- Two bamboo purse handles and gold hooks

INSTRUCTIONS

Lay out tan fabric and place ribbon in desired location. Using temporary adhesive or masking tape and pins, attach first ribbon to fabric, making sure it is even. Sew this ribbon to bag, stitching at top and bottom. Using same method, sew remaining ribbons to bag. Make sure ribbons are straight with ruler.

Sew bag together by folding in half right sides together, making sure ribbons match up. Sew side and bottom. To make flat bottom, sew diagonal stitch on each side of bottom seam (see Diagram A).

Sew black canvas right sides together, at top and bottom, like you did with tan fabric. Turn tan canvas piece right side out. Place black canvas piece right side out over top of tan fabric (so right sides are matching).

Cut four 2" pieces of polka dot ribbon and cut grosgrain ribbon in half. Fold each polka dot ribbon in half lengthwise. Pin each of these pieces to front and back of tan piece, 5" apart loop side down.

Pin each half of grosgrain ribbon directly in middle of each side of tan piece. Sew along top, removing pins as you go, making sure to catch ribbon in stitches. Leave 3" space for turning; turn right side out.

Iron top of bag and stitch finishing stitch around top of bag. Attach handles to hooks, and hooks to polka dot ribbon. Thread letter buttons with ribbon and tie to bag.

DIAGRAM A

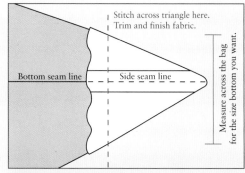

Stitch across triangle here. Trim and finish fabric.

Bottom seam line   Side seam line

Measure across the bag for the size bottom you want.

(Above) Spell out a friend's name with a bead and ribbon accent, a wonderful addition to this purse.

Any girlfriend with an affinity for purses will be enamored with this handmade ribbon purse. The plastic bamboo handles are available through many online stores.

91

Slice of Cake Box

MATERIALS

- Bone folder
- Exacto knife
- Glue stick
- Pencil
- Scissors
- Small gift
- Straight-edge ruler
- Two sheets 8 ½" x 11" cardstock, 1 for template, 1 for cake box
- Watercolors

INSTRUCTIONS

Photocopy pattern (page 95). Glue onto cardstock and cut out to create template.

Using pencil, trace around template onto cardstock "cake slice"; cut out shape. Score on all dotted lines using bone folder and ruler.

Cut slit for tab with Exacto knife. Paint and letter message on slice before assembling. Assemble; glue tabs. Add cake toppers, then insert gift.

(Left) Calligraphy beautifully delivers a birthday sentiment.

Expert Tip

Suggested cake toppers include:

- Buttons
- Calligraphy lettering
- Candle, small
- Curling ribbon
- Dried or silk flowers
- Glitter
- Hole punches
- Paint
- Puffy pen icing
- Ribbon
- Rickrack
- Sequins
- Trims

A small gift tucked inside this birthday box is a delightful surprise. Fill the box with shredded paper or wrap the gift in tissue paper and insert.

93

(Right) A few watercolor strokes and some colorful hole punches decorate the side of the cake slice, which is also embellished with a special message.

Girl Talk

A group of friends plotted for weeks to come up with the perfect theme for a friend's big birthday that ended with an "O". Party genius struck when the idea was hatched to ask each friend to visit the toy store and buy the Barbie doll she always wanted to be. Each guest came to the surprise party dressed as her Barbie. Her choice gave insight into her personality and the costumes were a great icebreaker to help everyone at the party get to know each other.

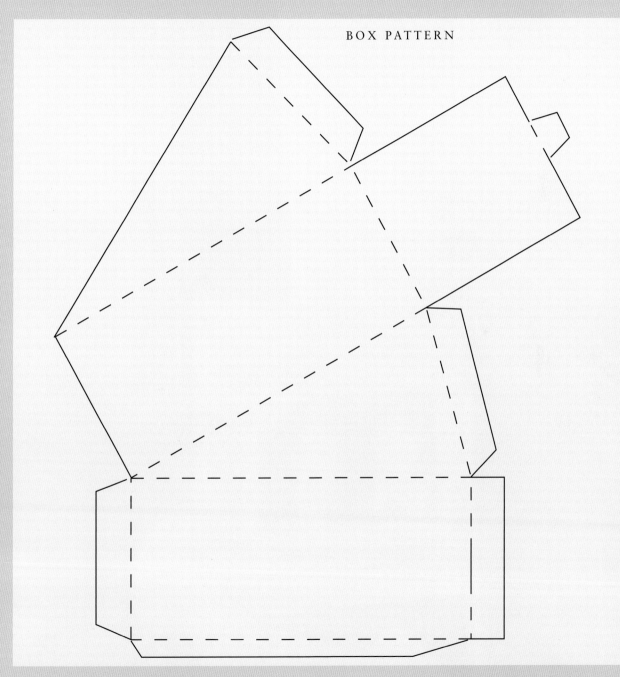

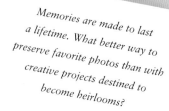

Memories are made to last
a lifetime. What better way to
preserve favorite photos than with
creative projects destined to
become heirlooms?

CHAPTER SIX

Memories of Us

"Treat your friends as you do your pictures and place them in their best light." —Jennie Jerome Churchhill

Pictures are often the footholds to which our memories cling. We all remember our dearest and oldest friends fondly, but often it takes a picture to transport us back to a specific moment in time. One look at an old photograph, and instantly we're 6 once more, treating our teddies to tea, or 13 and carefree, skating across the neighbor's pond arm-in-arm.

That's why when we go rummaging through a drawer and happen upon an old photo or two, it's a guaranteed reverie, a free ticket back in time to happiness past.

This chapter features ideas on how to gather these memories like the pearls they are, and then string them around at home, where they can scatter joy every day.

Whether you fashion something as utilitarian as a picture frame, or as decorative as a custom frame with a treasured photograph, you'll double your pleasure by making two— one to keep and one to give away. Just be sure to take Ms. Churchill's sage advice and choose your photographs wisely, putting only their best hair and makeup days out for display.

Friendship Tray

MATERIALS

- 8" x 10" decorative paper
- 8" x 10" wooden wall frame
- Four large buttons, with center indentations in design
- Four large decorative beads
- Glue stick
- Handheld electric or battery-driven drill and bits
- Hot glue gun
- One yard decorative trim or ribbon
- Strong-hold instant glue
- Two cabinet handles, with screws long enough to screw into handles

INSTRUCTIONS

Create page that expresses your sentiments using decorative papers, embellishments, and favorite photographs.

Remove glass from frame and affix each handle on opposite side of frame to create tray. Mount same way as you would on any cabinet front: by drilling holes and inserting screws from backside of frame. You may need to use longer screws than those that came with handles, depending on width of frame.

Replace glass in frame, insert decorated page, and firmly affix cardboard provided with frame back into place.

Cover back side of frame with decorative paper using glue stick. Hot glue decorative trim or ribbon to edges of paper.

Affix button at each back corner of tray using strong-hold instant glue. Once in place, glue large bead at center of each button.

Girl Talk

Who better than an old friend to remind you of ridiculous hairstyles, unflattering outfits, and old boyfriends? The magic of photographs is that you have proof to go with the stories! Imagine compiling the photographs with music, easily done on a computer, as one girlfriend did to surprise her friends.

Friendship is the theme of this picture frame-turned-tray that is sentimental and sophisticated.

Remember

A little bit of powder and a little bit of paint makes the old girl look like what she ain't.

I am letting my pores breathe!

GIRLFRIENDS

Picnic in the Park in Portland

True friendship is a no make-up day!

"THE ONLY GOOD TEACHERS FOR YOU ARE THOSE FRIENDS WHO LOVE YOU, WHO THINK YOU ARE INTERESTING, OR VERY IMPORTANT, OR WONDERFULLY FUNNY." —BRENDA UELAND

(Left) A large bead glued onto a button and secured with instant glue forms ornamental "feet" on the bottom of the tray. Scrapbook papers are used to finish the backside in style.

(Opposite page) Everyday cabinet handles serve a functional purpose on this tray. To attach, simply drill two holes and insert screws.

Remember

I am letting my pores breathe!

in the Park in Portland

make-up day!

Fantasy Boot Picture Frame

MATERIALS

- 1" craft brush
- 3D foam dots
- Bone folder
- Decoupage glue
- Favorite photo, photocopied
- Heavy cardstock
- Old book print pages
- Scissors

INSTRUCTIONS

Cut out paper elements (pages 104-105).

Decoupage one side of 8 ½" x 11" piece of heavy cardstock with old book print pages and back label. Turn over and decoupage picture frame element onto front; set aside to dry completely. Cut out entire picture frame.

Decoupage boot detail onto cardstock; set aside to dry completely, then cut out. Attach 3D foam dots to back of boot then adhere to frame. (Here two dots were used to create a greater dimensional effect.)

Gently score with bone folder along edge to make it stand. Decoupage photocopied photograph onto front of frame.

Girl Talk

There were four or five girlfriends who met in high school several years ago. The first year their circle of friends formed, they exchanged early childhood school pictures along with that year's class picture. Today they exchange pictures bearing the young faces of their own children, and watch the growth of each child rather than the aging of each other.

102

Decoupage your best friend's favorite childhood photo onto this picture frame for a very sweet gift.

103

"FORSAKE NOT AN OLD FRIEND, FOR A NEW
ONE DOES NOT COMPARE WITH HIM."
—ECCLESIASTICUS 9:10

Finish off the back of the frame
with lettering photocopied
from a century-old book.

BOOT DETAIL

BACK LABEL

ENLARGE 135%

Accordion Book

MATERIALS

- Brush-on glue (acid free)
- Brush-on pastels
- Decorative edge scissors
- Decorative papers and stickers
- Double-sided tape
- Embellishments such as small lettered plaques
- Exacto knife
- Photo corners
- Photographs sized to fit book
- Ruler
- Scrapbook brads, eyelets, and snaps
- Store-bought accordion book
- Straight edge scissors
- Two yards silk ribbon

INSTRUCTIONS

With straight edge scissors and ruler, cut decorative paper about ¼" larger on all sides than cover of accordion book.

Cover front and back of book with decorative paper using brush-on glue. Miter corners for finished look.

Lay silk ribbon on outside of back cover so front length of ribbon is same as back length; set in place with two scrapbook snaps at back. Embellish cover with small brass plaque (in this case the word "remember") and set in place with two scrapbook brads.

Affix pages to front cover by gluing top page to wrong side of front cover. Glue last page to wrong side of back cover.

Decorate pages by covering them with decorative papers, stickers, and other embellishments. Use double-sided tape when covering pages with paper so they do not warp. Tint edges of pages with brush-on pastels.

Affix photos same way. Use Exacto knife for clean cuts and to place stickers and photo corners. When finished, close book and tie closed with ribbon for presentation.

Remember

Fill your accordion keepsake with photos from your girlfriend's college graduation, wedding, an awards ceremony, or a special weekend away with best friends. (Opposite page) The accordion looks just as lovely open.

Scrapbook Pages Keepsake Box

MATERIALS

- Acrylic paint, cream
- Decoupage glue
- Felt
- Foam brush
- Hot glue gun
- Lint-free soft cloth
- Photographs
- Ribbon
- Rubber stamp and ink
- Sandpaper, 120 grit
- Scissors
- Scrapbooking papers, embellishments
- Square wooden box, at least 12" x 12"

INSTRUCTIONS

Lightly sand wooden box; wipe clean with cloth. With foam brush, paint wooden box; let dry completely. For worn appearance, lightly sand edges of box.

Decoupage cutouts, papers, and photographs to top of box; let dry. Add metal cutouts and rubber stamp wording as desired.

Cut felt in shape of pocket; attach with glue gun. Tie ribbon in bow and attach with glue gun.

(Left) To keep dimensional scrapbook pages intact, layer a piece of bubble packing material between each page.

Just as fun as the photos or scrapbook pages inside is this fanciful box adorned with endearing messages and treasured images.

FAMILY

FRIENDS

HAPPINESS & LOVE

sweet memories

Of MY life

Sometimes it's the sentiments of a handmade card or a thoughtfully wrapped gift that earns high marks for presentation.

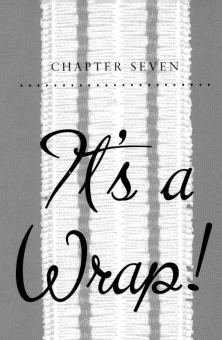

CHAPTER SEVEN

It's a Wrap!

*"We can do no great things—only small things
with great love." —Mother Teresa*

Like preparing a feast, in wrapping a gift you are creating a work of art that will endure for only a few fleeting moments. For this very reason, gift wrap is the perfect medium for trying daring new ideas.

When wrapping a gift for a girlfriend, let your imagination be your guide. Now's the time to pull out all your leftover crafting supplies, and that cache of odd and interesting items you just couldn't pass up at flea markets and antiques stores. If you have no such collection, you may want to start one—you'll find yourself looking with fresh eyes on boxes of buttons and scraps of vintage cloth you might otherwise have passed up.

As with any creative work, give yourself time to dream. Over a morning's cup of tea, sift through your supplies or pour over an art book. Note any color combinations or textural looks that strike your fancy.

Then dive in fearlessly—after all, no one turns down a gift because they don't like the wrap! You might let your girlfriend's interests be your guide, indulging her penchant for poodles or for pink with a wrap that's somewhat quirky or just downright girly. Or, use your wrap to suggest a mood—a scrap of Provencal fabric when you want something sunny or a few fallen twigs for a wrap that's all charming simplicity.

Wedding in a Bowl

MATERIALS

- Candle, cream or white
- Memory album
- Photo frame
- Scissors
- Sheer ribbon
- Silver bowl of your choice
- Tissue paper, white or cream
- Tulle
- Two dozen silk roses, white
- Two wine glasses

INSTRUCTIONS

Fill bottom of bowl with crumpled tissue paper. Arrange ⅔ of silk flowers atop filler at front of basket.

Carefully arrange memory album at back of bowl. Add candle, photo frame, and wine glasses, placing smallest items at front. Tuck in remaining silk roses to fill any empty spaces.

Roll out enough tulle to completely cover basket with excess left over for gathering and tying.

Bring sides of tulle up and over basket. Cut tulle few inches above basket. Gather wrap at top. Finish by tying ribbon around gathered tulle; tie bow at top.

(Above) Celebrate a dear friend's wedding with a thoughtful gift that will be remembered long after the "I Dos" are said.

Tulle holds items in place and creates an attractive, finished look to this wedding-themed gift.

Treasures Gift Wrap

MATERIALS

- Beads, assorted
- Decorative paper napkins
- Pinecone, gold
- Ribbon, gold-edged sheer, wire-edged metallic web, wire-edged sheer
- Scissors
- Tape
- Tissue paper
- Wire, small gauge
- Wrapping paper

INSTRUCTIONS

Small Box

Wrap gift box with wrapping paper. Tie gold-edged ribbon around gift and knot, leaving 42" tails. Tie bow; tie second bow offset from first bow. Tie third bow offset from first two bows.

Medium Box

Wrap package with wrapping paper. Separate top layer of napkin from back; discard back. Tear or cut napkin and adhere to top of package as desired. Thread beads on three lengths of wire strand as desired. Loosely twist wire strand and beads together. Wrap box with beaded wire, beginning in back. Wrap wire ends together at back of gift to secure.

Large Box

Wrap gift with tissue paper. Wrap web ribbon around box and tie knot to secure. Attach pinecone with craft wire. Attach four varying lengths of wire-edged sheer ribbon to web ribbon and tie bows.

Expert Tip

When it comes to wrapping gifts, some things to keep in mind:

- **Choosing gift wrap:** Consider the size of the box when picking out your gift wrap. Large, bold patterns are great for large boxes but won't look to scale on a small box.

- **Choosing ribbon:** Ribbon should be in proportion to your packages.

A thin ribbon looks best on small packages, while a wider ribbon creates a bigger bow, which is ideal for large packages.

- **Cutting ribbon:** Ribbon should always be cut at the ends diagonally or in an inverted "V" for a finished look.

- **Shipping gifts:** It's best to use wire ribbon, tulle, or yarn to avoid crushed or damaged bows.

- **Use double-sided tape:** For a clean look, wrap your gifts using double-sided tape.

Beads, baubles, ribbon, and even a pinecone make everyday extraordinary.

115

Easy-Open Gift Box

MATERIALS

- ¼" solid colored ribbon
- ¾" solid colored ribbon
- 2" sheer ribbon
- Blooms and berries
- Double-sided tape
- Floral foam
- Gift box
- Hot glue gun
- Plastic sheeting
- Scissors
- Silk flowers
- Wrapping paper

INSTRUCTIONS

Cut enough wrapping paper to cover box top, allowing additional ¼" to fold over box on each side; secure with double-sided tape. Repeat with bottom of box.

Attach 2" sheer ribbon to top of box, crossing at center and securing inside of box with tape. Layer with ¾" ribbon. Tie ¼" ribbon in bows on top center of box; attach silk flowers to center with hot glue gun.

Line inside of box with plastic sheeting. Soak floral foam in water and place inside box. Fill with favorite blooms and berries.

Girl Talk

. . . .

"From the time females are little girls, their mothers tell them to value their friendships with their girlfriends. When they become teenagers, and start to date boys, they often find themselves having to make choices. Perhaps they have promised a girlfriend on a Wednesday night they'll go to a Saturday night movie, but when a guy they have a crush on calls on Friday, they torture themselves trying to decide what to do. Some cancel with their girlfriends, justifying it on the grounds that they really like the guy. Their mothers shake their heads and say, 'The boys come and go, but your girlfriends are there forever.' That's something that's pretty hard to believe when you're a 16-year-old girl, but let me say that looking at it from the other end of the spectrum, it is so true." —Georgie Binks

By wrapping each piece of the gift box separately, you'll make opening it a cinch.

117

Fold-Out Card

(Above) *Neatly tucked through the card's ribbon tie is an antique silver charm.*

MATERIALS

- Floral trim
- Hot glue gun
- Metallic trim
- Pencil
- Pink metal eyelets and eyelet tools
- Pop dots
- Ruler
- Scissors
- Sewing machine
- Silk ribbon
- Silver charm
- Stickers
- Two patterned papers, pink and sage floral

INSTRUCTIONS

Trace 8" square onto both pieces of patterned paper; cut out.

Place wrong sides together and adhere to each other with sewing machine. Sew metallic trim to outside seam of envelope.

Set eyelet using eyelet tools in each corner of envelope. Place stickers on favorite image and attach to inside of card using pop dots.

Hot glue floral trim to inside edge of envelope. Thread silk ribbon through each eyelet. Tie ribbon together, threading silver charm through ribbon before tying into bow.

Girl Talk

Cards are given all the time. But there are very few that remain after a birthday or holiday. Such is the case with one card, featuring a group of zany women singing on the cover, given by one of four best friends. To this day, the card remains a treasured keepsake. It is a constant reminder of the decades-old friendships they share.

Sweet memories

FRIENDS

Scrapbooking embellishments send the perfect message to a best friend. The edges of this card are trimmed with a ribbon of silk flowers.

Fabric Greeting Cards

MATERIALS

- Brads
- Cardstock
- Decorative paper clip
- Embellishments, small frame and flower
- Fabric
- Hem tape
- Rubber stamp and ink
- Scissors
- Shipping tag, small
- Spray adhesive
- String

INSTRUCTIONS

Thank You Card

Fold cardstock in ⅓ of its width on the left and ⅔ its width on the right side. Cut and fray pieces of fabric to fit each side.

Apply spray adhesive to backside of fabric pieces; adhere to card fronts and let dry completely.

For more decorative touch, sew zigzag stitch around edges of fabric and add scrapbook page embellishments such as small frame shown here or flower.

Adhere brads to each flap of card and tie card closed with small piece of string. Rubber stamp greeting on small shipping tag and tie to third brad.

Happy Birthday Card

Fold sheet of cardstock in half and cut card to desired size. Cut one large square piece of fabric slightly smaller than front of card. Fray edges of fabric and sew onto card.

Rubber stamp greeting on paper, glue to strip of hem tape, and attach to card with decorative paper clip.

(Above) A small shipping tag rubber stamped sends a thank you message your girlfriend will surely remember.

Celebrate

Print greetings on a computer and add them to suit the occasion. Or, consider stamping your message or using rub-on letters.

happy birthday

121

Gift Tags

MATERIALS

- ¼" hole punch
- Fabric
- Ribbon
- Rubber stamp and ink
- Scissors
- Shipping tag or cardstock
- Trims
- White craft glue or spray adhesive

INSTRUCTIONS

If you do not have a shipping tag, create one by cutting piece of cardstock the desired size.

Lightly tack fabric with craft glue; let dry. Sew fabric onto tag with simple straight or zigzag stitches.

Adhere trims and ribbon to tag with craft glue.

Rubber stamp message onto tag. Punch hole at top of tag and thread through ribbon; tie in bow.

Girl Talk

Old photographs, color photocopied to save the original, were the inspiration for one girlfriend's gift tags. She simply cut out the images with decorative scissors and mounted each one to its own tag made from cardstock that was then hole punched and tied with a ribbon. The photos were a hit as the girls exchanged gifts and memories.

122

live

laugh

love

Shipping tags are available at most stationery and office supply stores and afford an array of personalizing possibilities.

to
from

Acknowledgments

Book Editor:
Catherine Risling

Contributor:
Katherine Anderson

Copy Editor:
Michele Hollow

Graphic Designers:
Deborah Kehoe,
*Kehoe + Kehoe Design
Associates, Inc.*
Burlington, VT
Lynn Lantz
David Walker

Photo Styling:
Rebecca Ittner
Catherine Risling

Photography:
Zac Williams
Ryne Hazen (pages 106-
107, 121, 123)
Denny Nelson (pages 2,
5, 11, 49, 62, 87)

Projects:
Destiny Stones
www.destinystones.com
Pages 34-35, 52-53, 84-87

Paige Hill
www.chapelleltd.com
Pages 20-21, 38-39, 46-
47, 54-55, 56-57, 74-75,
80-81, 86-87, 88-89, 90-
91, 108-109, 118-119,
120-121, 122-123

Paris Flea Market
Designs, Sandra Evertson
www.ParisFleaMarket
Designs.com
Pages 16-19, 26-29, 30-
33, 40-45, 64-67, 68-71,
76-79, 102-105

Eileen Cannon Paulin
www.redlips4courage.com
Pages 22-25, 98-101,
106-107

Janet Takahashi
www.chapelleltd.com
Pages 58-61, 72-73, 92-95

Aaron Brothers,
www.aaronbrothers.com

Anna Griffin,
www.annagriffin.com

Bazzill, available at local
craft and scrapbook
stores

C-Thru Ruler,
www.cthruruler.com

The Container Store,
www.containerstore.com

Darice, www.darice.com

Debbie Mumm,
www.debbiemumm.com

Delta,
www.deltacrafts.com

EK Success,
www.eksuccess.com

Fiskars, www.fiskars.com

French General,
www.frenchgeneral.com

Herma-fix, available at
local craft and scrapbook
stores

Hero Arts,
www.heroarts.com

Home Depot,
www.homedepot.com

IKEA, www.ikea.com

Inkadinkado,
www.inkadinkado.com

K&Company,
www.kandcompany.com

Making Memories,
www.makingmemories.com

Memories of a Lifetime,
available at local craft
and scrapbook stores

Mrs. Grossman's,
www.mrsgrossmans.com

Offray, www.offray.com

Plaid,
www.plaidonline.com

Stamp Craft, available at
local craft and scrapbook
stores

Stampendous,
www.stampendous.com

Susan Branch,
www.susanbranch.com

Universal Mercantile
Exchange, Inc.,
www.umei.com

Vintage postcard images
courtesy Kathy Alpert
and Postmark Press,
www.postmarkpress.com

Vintage ribbon supplied
by Tinsel Trading,
www.tinseltrading.com

Xyron, www.xyron.com

Page 16
FEEL GOOD SUGAR
COOKIES BOX
Fold-up box:
The Container Store

Page 20
VERY RELAXED
BATH SALTS
Small paint can:
Home Depot

Patterned paper:
Anna Griffin

Dimensional foam stickers:
K&Company

Flower and pink ribbon:
French General

Clear vellum: Bazzill

Clear embossing powder:
Stampendous

Page 22
MEMORIES OF
MOM JAR
Jar: IKEA

Page 30
BON BONS CANDY
CONTAINER
Glass canning jar:
The Container Store

Page 46
KINDRED SPIRITS
SCRAPBOOK COVER
Scrapbook with
photo frame:
K&Company

Rub-on words:
K&Company

Foam dimensional stickers:
K&Company

Page 54
THOSE WHO
MATTER JOURNAL
Patterned paper:
K&Company

Heart charm:
K&Company

Letter stickers:
K&Company

Vellum accented paper:
K&Company

Square tag:
Making Memories

Fibers: EK Success

Metal letters:
Making Memories

Metal tag letters:
EK Success

Letter stamps:
Hero Arts

Page 56
BOOKMARK SMART
Green cardstock:
Bazzill

Patterned paper:
K&Company

Stickers: K&Company,
Susan Branch

Buttons:
Making Memories

Fibers and ribbon:
Offray,
Making Memories

Laminating machine:
Xyron 510 and laminat-
ing cartridge

Circle hole punch: Fiskars

Paper trimmer: Fiskars

Temporary adhesive:
Herma-fix

Page 74
ANGEL EMBELLISHED
CANDLE
Letter stamps: Hero Arts,
Stamp Craft

Postmark stamps:
Inkadinkado

Brown tag:
French General

Jute thread: Darice

Padlock charm:
K&Company

Dotted ribbon: Offray

Page 80
GRADE-A CLIPBOARD
Vintage image:
Memories of a Lifetime

School stickers:
Debbie Mumm

Small letter stickers:
K&Company

Round letter stickers:
EK Success

Letter stamps:
Hero Arts, Stamp Craft

Ribbon: Offray

Twill word ribbon:
Making Memories

Decoupage medium:
Modge Podge by Plaid

Page 88
NOT JUST FOR
HATS BOX
White and green acrylic
paint: Delta

Metal charm:
K&Company

Metal letters:
Making Memories

Jute thread: Darice

Stencil tape: Delta

Page 90
RIBBON PURSE
Bamboo handles
and gold hooks:
Universal Mercantile
Exchange, Inc.

Ribbon: Offray

Page 98
BEST FRIENDS TRAY
Tray:
Aaron Brothers

Page 106
ACCORDION BOOK
Stickers and
embellishments:
K&Company,
Mrs. Grossman's

Page 118
FOLD-OUT CARD
Patterned paper:
Anna Griffin

Pink eyelets and
eyelet tools:
Making Memories

Envelope template:
C-Thru Ruler

Floral trim: Michaels

Vintage image:
Memories of a Lifetime

Stickers: K&Company

METRIC EQUIVALENCY CHARTS

inches to millimeters and centimeters
mm-millimeters   cm-centimeters

inches	mm	cm	inches	cm	inches	cm
1/8	3	0.3	9	22.9	30	76.2
1/4	6	0.6	10	25.4	31	78.7
1/2	13	1.3	12	30.5	33	83.8
5/8	16	1.6	13	33.0	34	86.4
3/4	19	1.9	14	35.6	35	88.9
7/8	22	2.2	15	38.1	36	91.4
1	25	2.5	16	40.6	37	94.0
1 1/4	32	3.2	17	43.2	38	96.5
1 1/2	38	3.8	18	45.7	39	99.1
1 3/4	44	4.4	19	48.3	40	101.6
2	51	5.1	20	50.8	41	104.1
2 1/2	64	6.4	21	53.3	42	106.7
3	76	7.6	22	55.9	43	109.2
3 1/2	89	8.9	23	58.4	44	111.8
4	102	10.2	24	61.0	45	114.3
4 1/2	114	11.4	25	63.5	46	116.8
5	127	12.7	26	66.0	47	119.4
6	152	15.2	27	68.6	48	121.9
7	178	17.8	28	71.1	49	124.5
8	203	20.3	29	73.7	50	127.0

yards to meters

yards	meters	yards	meters	yards	meters	yards	meters	yards	meters
1/8	0.11	2 1/8	1.94	4 1/8	3.77	6 1/8	5.60	8 1/8	7.43
1/4	0.23	2 1/4	2.06	4 1/4	3.89	6 1/4	5.72	8 1/4	7.54
3/8	0.34	2 3/8	2.17	4 3/8	4.00	6 3/8	5.83	8 3/8	7.66
1/2	0.46	2 1/2	2.29	4 1/2	4.11	6 1/2	5.94	8 1/2	7.77
5/8	0.57	2 5/8	2.40	4 5/8	4.23	6 5/8	6.06	8 5/8	7.89
3/4	0.69	2 3/4	2.51	4 3/4	4.34	6 3/4	6.17	8 3/4	8.00
7/8	0.80	2 7/8	2.63	4 7/8	4.46	6 7/8	6.29	8 7/8	8.12
1	0.91	3	2.74	5	4.57	7	6.40	9	8.23
1 1/8	1.03	3 1/8	2.86	5 1/8	4.69	7 1/8	6.52	9 1/8	8.34
1 1/4	1.14	3 1/4	2.97	5 1/4	4.80	7 1/4	6.63	9 1/4	8.46
1 3/8	1.26	3 3/8	3.09	5 3/8	4.91	7 3/8	6.74	9 3/8	8.57
1 1/2	1.37	3 1/2	3.20	5 1/2	5.03	7 1/2	6.86	9 1/2	8.69
1 5/8	1.49	3 5/8	3.31	5 5/8	5.14	7 5/8	6.97	9 5/8	8.80
1 3/4	1.60	3 3/4	3.43	5 3/4	5.26	7 3/4	7.09	9 3/4	8.92
1 7/8	1.71	3 7/8	3.54	5 7/8	5.37	7 7/8	7.20	9 7/8	9.03
2	1.83	4	3.66	6	5.49	8	7.32	10	9.14

Destiny Stones

Cassie Berrett, Brandy Shay, Tiffani Nye, and Rachelle Clausse share many things in addition to a love of jewelry. They are four sisters who together craft beautiful beaded pieces inspired by their mother, who always carried stones in her pockets because she believed in the metaphysical properties each one held. In their mother's memory, they started Destiny Stones, a purveyor of one-of-a-kind jewelry. Each semi-precious stone is hand picked and thoughtfully married to create unique necklaces, bracelets, and earrings. Destiny Stones jewelry is sold in retail stores throughout the United States and also is available through the Internet.

Sandra Evertson

Artist Sandra Evertson loves beautiful things, and thanks to her keen ability to see the magic in the ordinary, she is able to dream up extraordinary creations through the art of collage. Several years ago, Sandra began turning her collection of vintage papers into fanciful miniature theaters, bandboxes, ornaments, and art dolls. These original collages, which Sandra affectionately calls Posh Little Follies, reflect her affinity for turn-of-the-century papers, textiles, and photographs. Sandra is always seeking out vintage ephemera, from 19th-century postcards to magazines published during the 1800s. Sandra is the author of "Fanciful Paper Projects: Making Your Own Posh Little Follies." Sandra's work can also be seen in "Memories of a Lifetime—Weddings," "Instant Memories—Babies," and "Where Women Create."

Paige Hill

Paige Hill has always been a creative soul. As a child, her favorite activities included crafting something for a season or special event. Whether decorating for the holidays or helping Mom with pinecone wreaths, something artistic was always going on. In college, she studied fashion merchandising and worked in retail sales. She married and together she and her husband are raising three children. Along the way Paige has been in business with her parents teaching craft classes and selling handcrafted items to gift and interior design stores. Paige is a freelance craft designer, creating craft projects for many great books, including "Designer Scrapbooks with April Cornell" and "Designer Scrapbooks The Red Hat Society Way." She also is the author of "Scrapbooking Life's Celebrations."

Eileen Cannon Paulin

Ever since she can remember, Eileen Cannon Paulin has been fond of knitting, sewing, decoupaging, and just about any other handicraft she's seen as intriguing. She studied writing in college and has been able to combine her head with her heart's desires as a home décor magazine editor and now a book publisher. She is the author of "The Serene Home" and "Decorating for the First Time." Eileen is the founding girlfriend behind Red Lips 4 Courage Communications, Inc., a publishing services company that specializes in conceptualizing, writing, and producing hardcover books for women, about women. Eileen's great aunt Alida Hagerty, the picture of sweet confection, is the inspiration for her company's name. Hospitalized for an ailment no family member can recall, Alida was true to form when she greeted Eileen's cousin, Lynda, in a pink lace bed jacket and a smile on her face. When Lynda asked if she'd like to take a walk, her aunt fumbled through her purse, opened her lipstick, and applied a fresh coat of color. Looking Lynda in the eye she said, "Red lips for courage—that's what I always say!"

Janet Takahashi

Janet Takahashi has mastered several forms of visual arts including calligraphy, illustration, bookbinding, sign painting, and gilding. She is an avid journal keeper, filling art note pads in a precise, orderly manner using letterforms typically reserved for master calligraphers. Her ardent ability to combine calligraphy with illustrations and gilding defines many of her art pieces. Her most impressive accomplishments include restoring an old Clymer Printing Press (circa early 1800s), painstakingly restoring 12 volumes of vintage magazines and compiling them into a hand-bound book, and the gilding of a replica of the Palace of Versailles.

Index

AT THE OPERA